SPECTRUM

A COLLECTION OF POEMS

ANANYA DAHIYA

ISBN 979-888591021-7

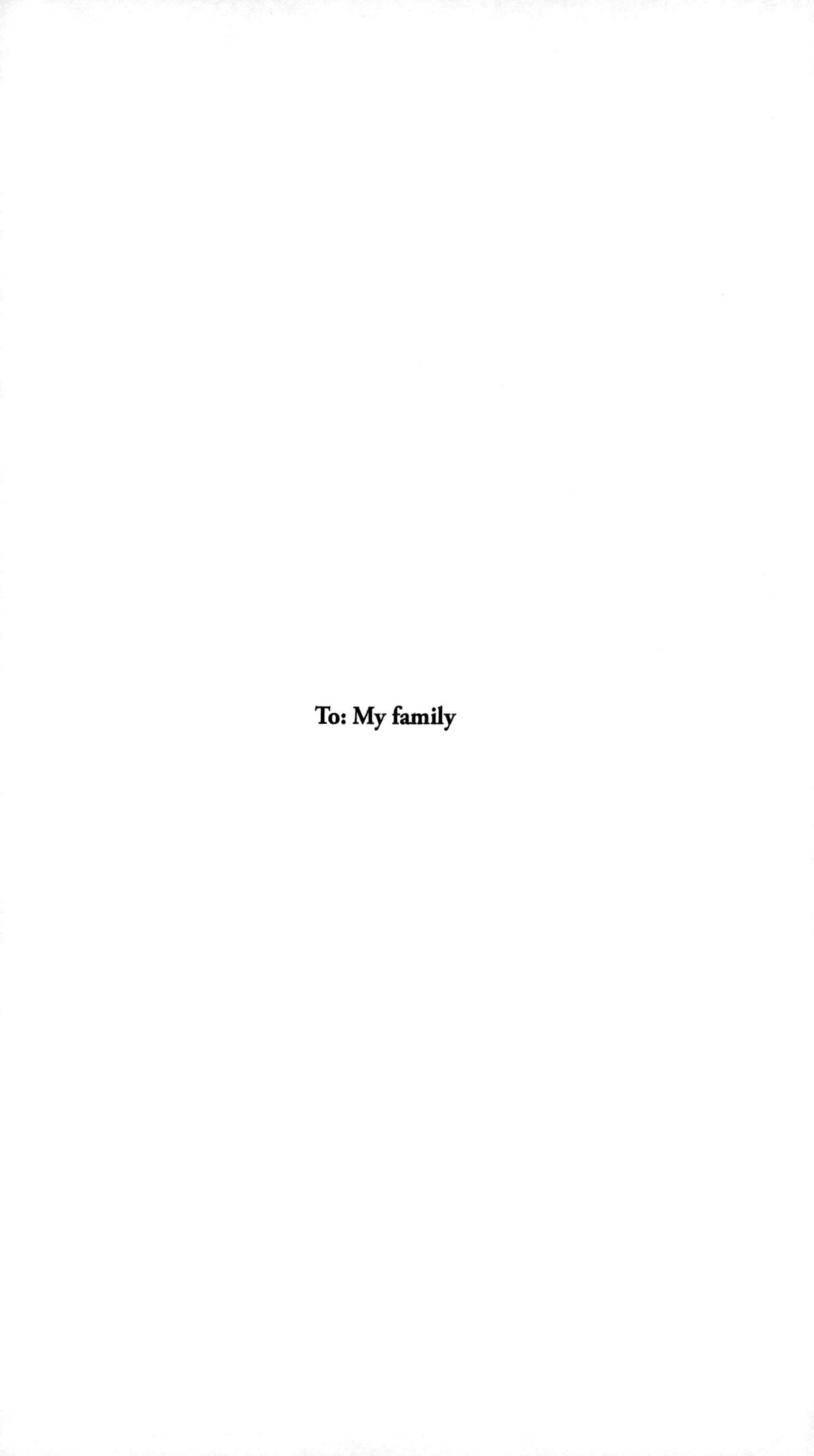

To: My family

Contents

Contents

Preface

Dear reader,

Everything in this world takes a price, and so has this book. I have been passionately publishing stories and poems in other anthologies but, this is my first personal title. My efforts are to inverse the dispersion process so that every school of thought in a spectrum turns out into white pages. Since I presented every emotion of the mind, this book will speak to different topics. It may be philosophy, or it may be fantasy. Or it may be about sports you will read. A mingling of humour and thrill in between will keep you entertained. However, the first part and foremost poem of this book are about my experience conveying my messages to leaves.

I hope you will enjoy it,

Ananya

Acknowledgements

I would love to put the foundation brick of the book by expressing my gratitude to someone special. My life, my younger brother, Anirudh, you are as gifted as stubborn you are. Your dedication in teasing me granted inspiration.

I‘m thankful to my maternal grandmother, Usha Dhaundiyal. Those nights I contributed to my poems, she was the one to care for me.

People say a man is a kite and that string that makes it fly is its family. My parents Krishna Dhaundiyal and Krishan Dahiya. From the core of my heart, I present my regards to you. Your support was essential for me. Only with your blessings, my poems purified crystal clear.

My aunt, Kapila Dhaundiyal, is as caring as my mother. The naming of this book is only possible by your diligence. Your every word for me consisted of motivation. You are the one who guides me whenever I want to flourish my passion. I have a special thankful feeling for you.

I'm obliged to my uncles, Biresh Dhaundiyal and Ravinderjeet Singh. They are the ones who reviewed and revived the actual potential of my poems. If I were appointed to award Nobel Prizes, the literature was one-sided to both of them.

Thank you, my cousins, who are more like siblings. Param Kaur, Raavi Kaur, Kavya Dhaundiyal, Parth Dhaundiyal, Tejaswini Dhaundiyal and Yuvraj Dhaundiyal. Your playfulness kept me writing for children.

Rahim Das once wrote "If teacher and God are both in front of me, who will I greet first? He then says it is only because of the teacher's teaching that I am able to see God."
Ms Mansi Tayal, I will immortal your teachings in my titles. This book is only possible by your attention towards me. You sharpened my talent and explained to me what am I capable of. My Hindi teacher, Ms Uma Sharma, although this book is in English, I have been obedient to our 'Sanskriti'. Please accept my gratitude.

The secret of my positive spirit is safe with the other literature teachers to whom I'm thankful. Ms Megha Arora, Ms Punam Munjal, and Ms Preety Soloman thank you for boosting my confidence.

"School is not only the end but the beginning of education.", Calvin Coolidge's words proved that school is not only a building but actually a holy place to be worshipped. My sincere appreciation to Maharaja Agarsain Public School, and Queen Mary's School. They taught me to make decisions in my life and nurtured me into an independent individual.

My last expression of gratitude, but not the least is to you dear reader. I will effort my best to communicate the deepest knowledge I have with my words.

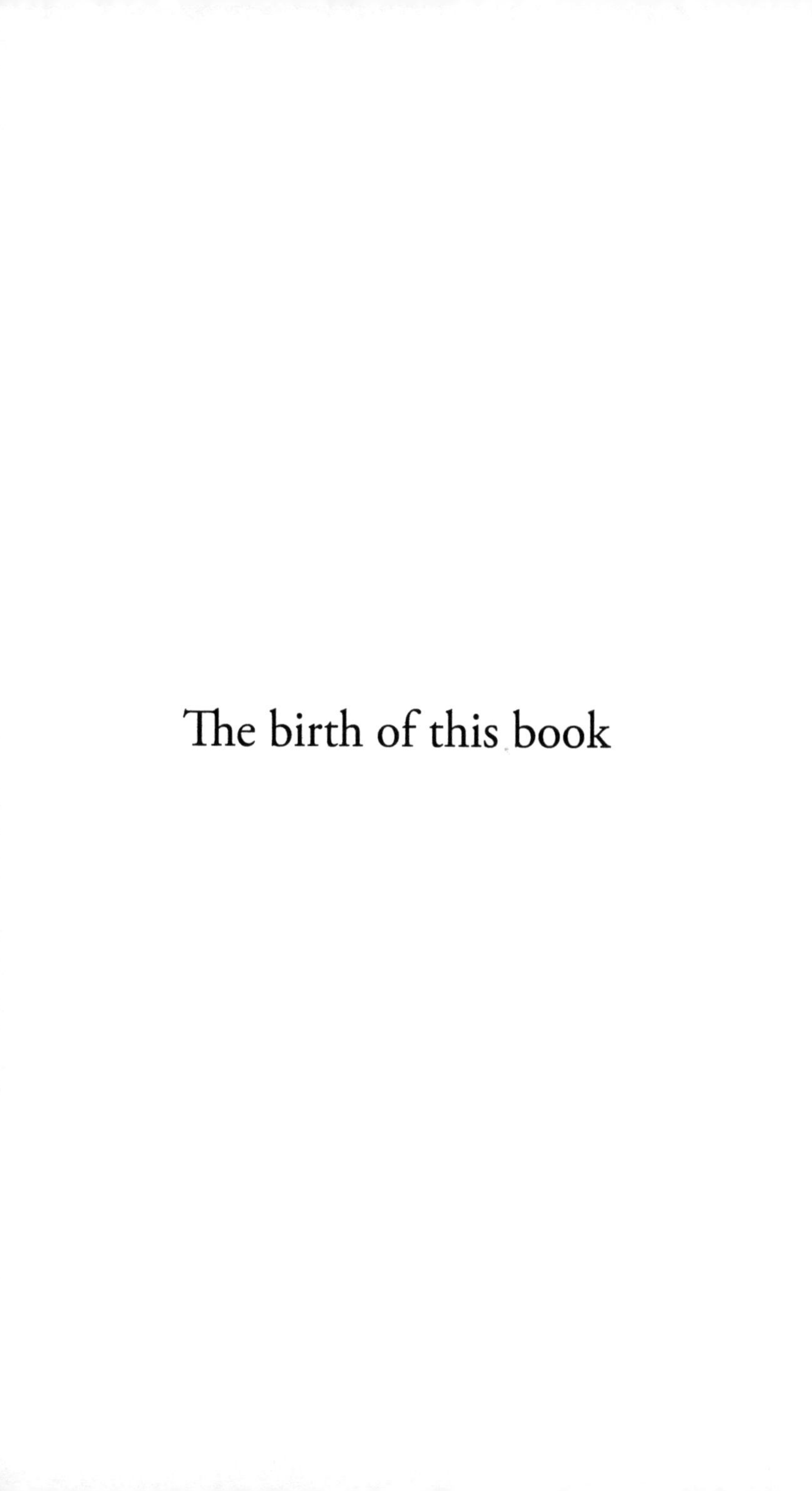

The birth of this book

1. The sleepless dream nights

Under that pitch-black atmosphere,
will enlight a lantern of know knowledge,
when my heart and body will become one,
seeking the most luxurious vocabulary as a mortgage.

Under that dumb atmosphere,
propagandas we will spawn,
for nights the Gemini will unite,
and pigment black on white until dawn.

Where my restless heart will flitter stories,
and the body argue with them,
where similarity piles countless inventories,
infinite stanzas we may design.

That night when eye bags become caffeine conscious,
Two lovers will unite after a wait of years,
one lubricious and other mercurial,
to this book, they will pour their tears.

Not every piece of paper guarantees happiness,
it may be money, folklore or abstract,
but even to a non-living rock, it may employe dizziness,
when it's that body and this heart.

Philosophy

2. Imperfectness is a norm

The ruler of avifauna,
this green essence on your blue gown,
and your go crown more lustrous than Sultana,
from your eyes, why do these diamonds drown?

Oh, my melodious minister,
how mysteriously colours mingle in my cape,
my charisma in the rain is peculiar,
then why do I deserve witch's feet for my shape?

Your majesty, imperfectness is a norm,
what you receive depends on what you give,
when your legs deform,
so charming and royal you live.

Explore me, your majesty,
I can't even build my nest,
where my parenting tended nasty,
still, my voice pleases every ear to best,

Everything is beautiful when you want,
but the desire is the deepest ocean,

what you want will forever taunt,
but what you have is the actual celebration.

3. Divine beauty

So much difference,
yet so same,
such a divine beauty,
exists in god's name.

The Greek god Zeus,
the Indian god Indra,
both are kings,
both control thunder-lightnings.

Gautam Buddha and Jesus Christ,
the incarnations of god,
same they preached about living life,
both of their thinking broad.

That ultimate power,
the blinding light,
every religion hover,
the difference exists despite.

The difference of his outfits,
the difference of preaches he gives,

the difference exists due to different aspects,
the beauty is the sole almighty who forgives.

4. The unexplained poem

The book, which read as a tale of love,
this society burned it down,
the beautiful flapping dove,
they caged it down.

Tears of that dove,
those burning pages,
its scream echoed,
throughout the mountain ranges.

The moon was dull as if it was new,
those beautiful red walls wearing,
this voice understood by few,
whereas many are hearing.

That book is my eye,
those walls are my lips,
the burning pages are personified,
to describe my wet eye tips.

People speak to express,
but I vocalize to aware,

the feeling that society suppressed,
that I exist here.

5. Definition of life

Sleep is history,
the dream is a mystery,
the goal is the source of oxygen,
which is the tree.

Life is chemistry,
you are chlorine,
Search for your mate sodium,
and become carefree.

One, two, three,
are you left with some valency,
are you saturated,
or your heart is left for me?

6. Struggle

Who forgets those moments,
instead victories people display,
redirecting your attention from current,
to the unnoticed dark side play.

A game of business, between death and clock,
one side match this is, you are bound to live,
an open-ended question, not very mock,
your answer to success, you are bound to give.

Society is not a friend or foe,
where is that great war of passion and profession,
they examine you from tip to toe,
and here you are trapped in this insane situation.

Kill your heart and get their praise,
its a doe or die in this cliffhanger,
from generation to generation disciplines this case,
when youth explores the world to kill their hunger.

7. The noble of the nobles

Love, disciplines, guidance and care,
I found everything in a single person,
the superior occupation they have,
without them, there is no profession.

They write in black and white,
but bring colours to my life,
the scold me when I'm wrong,
but are proud of me when I'm right.

Every day we go to the holy place: school,
worship them more than god,
whose knowledge is more than the bible,
because the teacher only proved the existence of the almighty lord.

8. My love, my mom

She was mine,
and will always be,
she was my birthright,
and will be until I die.

A true love,
and true kiss,
when she will away from me,
she will always miss.

I will remember her curly black hair,
sieving sunlight coming over me,
I wish she is always there,
but could she always be?

9. I want it more

Give me some more,
I wish I could drink it all,
Please a bit more,
So that I never reach to god.

I never hesitated to live,
Neither I feared to die,
Now that I met you,
I want to immortal as claimed in folklore,
For goodness sake, a half glass more.

How will I ever forget the taste?
Murder people and making my life waste?
That was a crime,
Man, It was in my life I faced.

A few measures, not more, I will praise,
So that, with this offence, I can space.

Sports

10. A bat in my hands

Now is my turn,
will I be a duck,
or my account will have,
a couple of runs.

The ball is mine,
shall I flick it,
let it go helicopter,
or straightway six it.

I stroked the ball towards the wicketkeeper,
I started to run,
I noticed I was out,
still, my mind was in doubt,
the umpire crossed his on his chest,
and shook his head,
I immediately took roundabout.

It is the starting of the nervous nineties,
Oh! Bowler, please don't lick it,
I wish it doesn't end as googly,

I will not be able to hit it.

Announcements took place,
I was the man of the match,
our team won the trophy
we were the all-time best batch.

11. India, my soul

From east to west,
from all of its rest,
from T-20 to test,
India is the best.

From vegetable to fruit,
from shoot to root,
from hair to boot,
India is awfully cute.

From the master to the mistress,
from robes to dress,
from hockey to chess,
India is always more,
never less.

12. Kick-Volleyball

It starts with love all,
and end with twenty-one,
no matter short or tall,
sometimes, the shorter can be the tricky one.

Use your knee, shoulder, toes and head,
to hit the ball yellow and red,
if the hand you use,
one point you will use.

At a time, three players,
two players are rare,
compete with a team of fifteen,
if your dare.

If your pass is accurate,
you can win the match,
either early or late,
but if it is outside the court,
lose your point like a boat from a port.

Fantasy

13. Snow princess

Her gown was as white as snow,
her skin is fair bright,
her eyes filled with darkness,
the darkness which can never enlight.

Her heart can never be warm,
only fire can end her storm,
she never tried to harm,
neither she is calm.

Her home is in the middle of nowhere,
still, she is a nomad,
one can never come near her,
still, everyone inside her she had.

No, she is not a ghost,
neither she is alive,
she is borns,
and she dies.

She needs a host,
as cold as her to survive,

someday in fire,
she has to dive.

14. The matchless trek of Vaishno Devi

The rising path was steep,
blooming to ravish till the end,
a staff they were instructed to keep,
and walk while they bend.

An enthusiast teen,
motioned rigidly but was keen,
as if local to this miraculous land,
where every step is protected by a magical hand.

On every half a kilometre,
she paused on a bench,
things became good to better,
when her father bought her to munch.

Her brother was hardly on his back,
when she chased a dog very black,
constantly three kilometres they ran,
but sat halfway, waiting for members from their clan.

The auspicious crossroad became dense,
but the siblings managed to wrap,
a single path focused by their natural lense,
until they found their parents walking.

A Series of drastic happenings took place,
more challenging than a mental maze,
the parents walked the average length,
where the girl pays off every strength.

A tear appeared in her eyes,
but she pulled them up,
until that magical hand gave her a surprise,
on her destination, she ended up.

How glamour this goddess appear,
whose dangling jewels she struggled to see,
how kindly Maa never let her tear,
whose trek was now obstacle-free.

15. My twin

Whenever I felt lonely,
I opened up to him,
to the boy in the mirror,
appearing in reflective surfaces solely.

He claims to be my twin,
but my mom never noticed him,
no one else sees him,
neither I'm like him.

At times he is nasty,
he sinks out of the mirror,
whenever I weep,
and makes me cry louder.

Slapping me on my face,
he laughs in that case,
I concluded this was a mental disorder,
remembering when I was a toddler.

When I saw him first,
he was nice to me,

but evil came next,
now I'm surviving this violence.

I thought I had to bear it till death,
when of sudden he pulled me off my bed,
and stuffed me into the mirror,
which he had left.

Now, I'm the boy in the mirror,
stuck inside here,
I follow him everywhere,
to prove that real me is in here.

Alas, everyone found me up there,
former boy in mirror stays where.

16. That deal with devil

On a mountain road,
I was playing for dear life,
expected to fight out dangerous load,
to reach to that other side of the knife.

Now I live to regret,
dealing this deal with the devil,
but beggars are not to select,
so I ceased my mouth before it is ravile.

Listlessly and aimless, I mooched,
a half trunk creature cautioned me,
heading towards me like to furiously smooch,
I hid behind green climbers freakingly.

It was confused extinct Phiomia,
followed by two trunked Gompotherium,
I sneaked as those bumpy creatures bumped,
was it hell or an elephant vivarium?

Where both those creatures struggled u-turning,
a Mammoth appeared backwards,

I who was behind them noticed it running,
I quickly climbed these climbers.

It's rude to call that satisfying,
as that trio fell off the cliff,
a complex of emotions my mind implying,
unaware that the next danger might be.

A red man in black underwear,
laughed maniacally at me,
spraying laughing gas everywhere,
his aim was the same as those three.

I moonwalked petrified,
until I fell on a herb,
laugh proof that certified,
and that red man was on my curb.

It was the devil himself,
and my need to hide in his glass palace,
if I won they offer me a dine,
otherwise, I will lose my life with this race.

The two minutes of judgement,
I motioned for the sake of life,
he discovered me in the lavatory regiment,
thank god two minutes already thrived.

17. A letter to Covid-19

David-o-David19,
am I your nephew,
then why this torturing quarantine,
and this revenging curfew?

One Christmas letter I forgot writing,
I realize it was yours,
first Christmas, you gifted grounding,
and that other one made me do chores.

Such a playback you plotted,
for a fault, I never knew,
for a warm welcome outside, cops scouted,
and where my parents now love me true.

You made me do maths,
such a massive death count,
from Ms Positive to Mr Test,
nothing more can ever haunt.

David-o-David 19,
please somewhere you disappear,

before I turn thirteen,
go and prevent my fatty layer.

18. Medusa

Dare to fight her,
her hair will grab you,
hold of her blonde hair,
you will turn weak and blue.

Like chameleon they are,
green, blonde, blue,
they even change their size,
depending on how far are you.

Medusa is the X- factor of her team,
She is the herald of a safe world,
very charming and adorable,
no sign of weakness,
neither she is vulnerable.

One day, she faced Trapster,
with his power, who stuck her emerald blue hair,
her hand went inside her waist bag,
with her blade, she cut off her sticky layer.

He kicked,

she hissed,
she picked him up with her hair,
and tossed him down,
he screamed a painful groan.

He started back paddling,
his other palm on his hinge,
he muttered something,
and left stumbling.

That was the end of the adventurous fight,
but not the joy of her life,
she lived with satisfaction,
but with continued heroic strife.

19. A broad tale

One night very merry,
I was walking on the street,
the sky was blueberry,
stars like shining popcorns,
ready to eat.

That celestial rice-cake was snow-white,
when that woman appeared,
time-worn but face competing with moonlight,
her spine bent with age,
ironic her eyes sapphire.

Where are you going, madam,
I asked her, in a tone very gentle,
gradually at me, eyes made a room,
I'm heading to the next street,
she replied with a chuckle.

"Oh madam, please let me lift you there,
you seem very tired.",
to what she answered, "think twice before this decision you drew,
what will happen if you regret it in future,

from your commitment; if you endeavoured."

I assured her and lifted her weight,
since heavy dumbells, I was used to picking,
just a few steps away from other streets before I isolate,
but suddenly it left far away,
Moreover, her sudden increase in pounds made me flick.

An eternity reared a minute,
when the background blacked,
our direct transportation in park horrified dilute,
with that woman acquired a constant mass,
and on my spine, she sacked.

She departed from my back,
and from nowhere, a hammer got in her hand,
I redied to run before she made attempts to smack,
until she held a nail,
and started hammering inside the land.

"Oh, gentleman, very kind,
no greediness you subsume,
as pure as a crystal is your mind,
I express my gratitude to you,
collect your treasure, may happily your life resume."

My eyes opened with a flash,

it was not a dream but a vision,
I dug where money mined out in a gush,
my life became much perfect,
with that extraordinary fusion.

20. That lady in the painting

It's unknown that canvas painted for how long,
by appearance is that to renaissance it belongs,
from generation to generation it succeeds along,
until the painting was lost by the guardian, it wrongs.

Earth green background and a pale lady in a gown,
a dog companies her with chubby skin and furs brown,
that woman who naturally tattoed by a frown,
she is the most benevolent to the death crown.

With blood is performed her manicure,
and with an appendix, her hair secure,
for dinner, she feeds a human mature,
her radio substituted by her cruel folklore.

That lady in the painting,
the only appointment you can have is in the evening,
when she is out of frame walking,
otherwise, strictly never hope for surviving.

Once a poet discovered her lot,
and showed up to poem-jot,
he was as daring to taunt,
until that lady appeared to haunt.

Like an eye, she souped that night,
and noddle his intestine despite,
gaining knowledge about my identity you may fright,
my soul is the one trapped to serve her inside.

21. Memories

In the corner of this world,
when I was busy cleaning,
accidentally, I removed the dust,
from my childhood dreaming.

My heart sunk in those kiddish doodles,
and those big clumsy alphabets,
I found my shiny little marbles,
and those trading cards I won during bets.

The fading memories rediscovered with age,
as the photos flash- forwarded me,
how I used to play with old tyres,
and fly aeroplanes in the breeze.

From the deepest ocean,
my memories recreated,
when when I noticed my first medal,
which became very much celebrated.

The teenage days were exotic,
followed by youth days charming,

and my first salary came in hand,
my childhood was gradually electroplating.

The big day of my life,
when I got married to my wife,
and we were blessed with our child,
from then, I settled mild.

Looking my daughter marry,
in her arms, I cried,
such a wonderful kid she is,
supported me when her mother died.

From that electroplated childhood,
that silver washed out clear,
from metal, I feel like fluid,
and from relationships untied.

9 798885 910217

Printed by Libri Plureos GmbH in Hamburg, Germany